How are they the same?

Bobbie Kalman

🌳 Crabtree Publishing Company

www.crabtreebooks.com

Created by Bobbie Kalman

Author and Editor-in-Chief
Bobbie Kalman

Educational consultants
Elaine Hurst
Joan King
Jennifer King

Notes for adults
Jennifer King

Editors
Kathy Middleton
Crystal Sikkens

Design
Bobbie Kalman
Katherine Berti

Print and production coordinator
Katherine Berti

Prepress technician
Katherine Berti

Photo research
Bobbie Kalman

Photographs
Photos.com: page 13 (top)
Other photographs by Shutterstock

Library and Archives Canada Cataloguing in Publication

Kalman, Bobbie, 1947-
    How are they the same? / Bobbie Kalman.

(My world)
Issued also in electronic format.
ISBN 978-0-7787-9556-8 (bound).--ISBN 978-0-7787-9581-0 (pbk.)

    1. Animals--Miscellanea--Juvenile literature. 2. Visual
perception--Juvenile literature. I. Title. II. Series: My world
(St. Catharines, Ont.)

QL49.K3325 2011   j590   C2010-907434-3

Library of Congress Cataloging-in-Publication Data

Kalman, Bobbie, author.
 How are they the same? / Bobbie Kalman.
      p. cm. -- (My world)
  ISBN 978-0-7787-9581-0 (pbk. : alk. paper) -- ISBN 978-0-7787-9556-8
(reinforced library binding : alk. paper) -- ISBN 978-1-4271-9663-7
(electronic (pdf))
  1. Animals--Miscellanea--Juvenile literature. I. Title. II. Series.

  QL49.K293185 2008
  590--dc22

                                                2010047121

Crabtree Publishing Company

www.crabtreebooks.com   1-800-387-7650

Printed in China/022011/RG20101116

Published in Canada
Crabtree Publishing
616 Welland Ave.
St. Catharines, Ontario
L2M 5V6

Published in the United States
Crabtree Publishing
PMB 59051
350 Fifth Avenue, 59th Floor
New York, New York 10118

Published in the United Kingdom
Crabtree Publishing
Maritime House
Basin Road North, Hove
BN41 1WR

Published in Australia
Crabtree Publishing
386 Mt. Alexander Rd.
Ascot Vale (Melbourne)
VIC 3032

Words to know

different

dinosaur

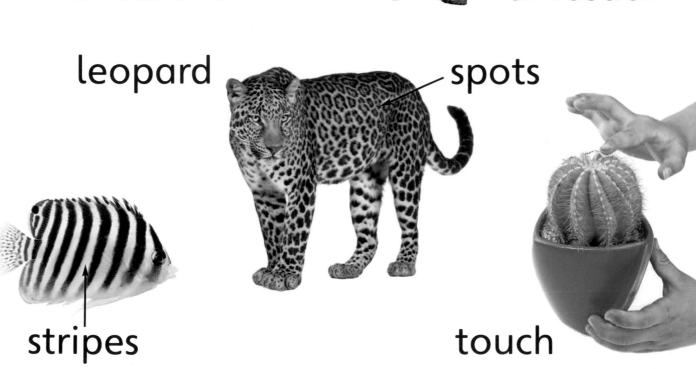

leopard

spots

stripes

touch

These animals are the same.
How are they the same?
They are also **different**.
How are they different?

The animals all have **stripes**.
Stripes are lines that repeat.
What colors are their stripes?

This cat is a **leopard**.
A leopard has **spots** on its coat.

How are these animals the same as a leopard? Are they cats, too?

leopard butterfly

leopard gecko

leopard frog

How are these things the same?
How do they feel
when you **touch** them?

pine needles

porcupine fish

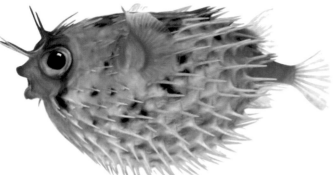

hedgehog

cactus

How can you tell that
they would feel the same?

Some of these animals are the same.
How are they the same?

One of these animals is different.
Which one is it?
How is it different from the others?

How are these animals the same?
What is each one doing?

duck

crocodile

chicken

snake

Did you guess that
each one is coming
out of an egg?

What is in
this egg?

Activity

What kind of animals are these?

Velociraptor

Talarurus

Stegosaurus

Which **dinosaur**
on the other page
looks most like
the Stegosaurus?

Aucasaurus

Which dinosaur
looks most like
the Aucasaurus?

15

Notes for adults

Objectives
- to have children identify similarities and differences in animals
- to teach children about similarities and differences in patterns, textures, body parts, actions, and kinds of animals

Before reading the book
Have the children bring in stuffed animals. Discuss the similarities and differences in how the animals look.

Tell the children to look at the cover of the book and ask these questions:

"Which animals do you see on the cover?"

"How are they the same?"

"Are the patterns on their bodies similar or different?" (Explain that patterns are lines and colors that repeat.)

"How are their sizes different?"

"How else are they different?" (Elicit differences such as wings, number of legs, their body coverings, how the animals move, and whether they spend their time on land, in water, or in the sky.)

After reading the book
"Which animals have stripes?" (zebra, bird, butterfly, tiger cub, fish)

"What do the leopard butterfly, leopard gecko, and leopard frog all have?" (spots)

"How are the pine leaves, porcupine fish, hedgehog, and cactus similar?" (sharp texture)

"Which animals on pages 10-11 have wings?" (butterfly, duck, ladybug, bat)

"Which one does not have wings?" (the dog)

Introduce the word "hatch" to the children.

"Which animals are hatching from eggs?" (duck, crocodile, chicken, snake)

Activity: Classification
Set up chart paper with these headings: stripes, spots, small, big, sharp, eggs, wings, dinosaurs, and plants

Ask the children to name the animals or plants in the book that belong to each group. Then ask the children to draw pictures of at least one animal that matches each category.

Extension
The following books will help children expand their understanding of colors, shapes, sizes, patterns, similarities, and textures.

Author Bobbie Kalman:

What color is it?

What shape is it?

How does it look?

How does it feel?

Is it big or small?

Is it the same or different?

Guided reading: J

For teacher's guide, go to www.crabtreebooks.com/teachersguides